I is for IOWA

I is for IOWA

Written by
Mary Ann Gensicke

Illustrated by
Lonna Nachtigal

IOWA STATE UNIVERSITY PRESS/AMES

MARY ANN GENSICKE received her BA in elementary education from the University of Iowa and her MA in library science from the University of Northern Iowa. A former elementary schoolteacher and a member of the Cedar Rapids Area Reading Council and the Iowa Reading Association, she is presently a media specialist for the Cedar Rapids Community School District.

LONNA NACHTIGAL is a freelance designer and illustrator and lives on a small farm near Ames, Iowa.

Photographic acknowledgments appear at the end of the book.

© 1995 Iowa State University Press, Ames, Iowa 50014, except for all line art: © 1995 Lonna Nachtigal

♾ Printed on acid-free paper in the United States of America

First edition, 1995
Second printing, 1996

Library of Congress Cataloging-in-Publication Data

Gensicke, Mary Ann
        I is for Iowa/written by Mary Ann Gensicke; illustrated by Lonna Nachtigal.
                p.   cm.
        Summary: Illustrations and text representing each letter of the alphabet present information about geographical locations, important industries, significant historical events, and extraordinary people in the state of Iowa.
        ISBN 0-8138-2404-4
        1. Iowa—History—Juvenile literature. 2. English language—Alphabet—Juvenile literature. [1. Iowa—History. 2. Alphabet.] I. Nachtigal, Lonna, ill. II. Title.
F621.3.G46   1995
977.7—dc20   95-15837

To all of the children
who pass through or live between the
boundaries of this bountiful state

This book was written in memory of
my mother, who taught me to love and
appreciate my heritage. She believed
that there is no place
on earth more
beautiful than Iowa—
with its acres of green forests and
farmlands that turn into autumn
patchworks of fiery color, only to become
clothed in winter's whitest garments.

Welcome to Iowa's rich history!

Aa

is for

Amana Colonies

The colonies are a group of seven villages that were first settled by German craftsworkers and scholars who held common religious beliefs. Today the colonies are world famous for their old-world traditions. They are a national historic landmark and Iowa's leading visitor attraction.

Bb
is for

Black Hawk

4

Black Hawk was a famous Sauk Indian chief who was brave and intelligent. He wanted to live on land that belonged to his ancestors. Iowa is known as the "Hawkeye State" in his honor.

Cc is for computer

John Atanasoff

Clifford Berry

The first computer was invented by John Atanasoff and Clifford Berry at Iowa State University. Computers have changed a lot since they were first built. Now, they are part of our everyday lives—from our cars, to the computers you use in school, to those used in industry.

Dd
is for
Dubuque

Julien Dubuque was the first white man to settle in Iowa.

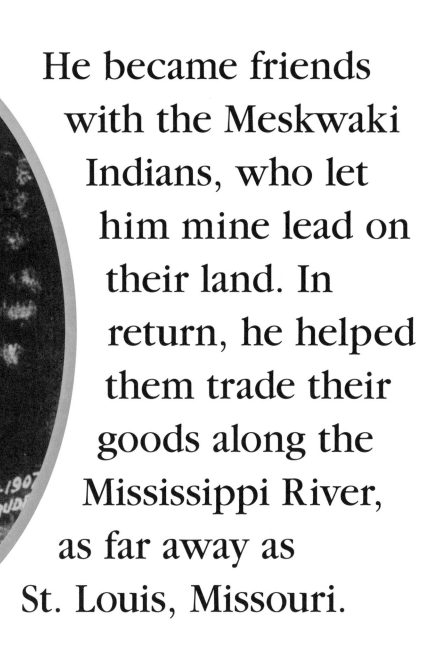

He became friends with the Meskwaki Indians, who let him mine lead on their land. In return, he helped them trade their goods along the Mississippi River, as far away as St. Louis, Missouri.

Ee

is for

Eskimo Pie

6 BARS 2.5 FL OZ EA (75 mL EA) 15 FL OZ (450

Dark Chocolate Coating – Vanilla Ice Cream

This ice cream treat, invented in 1921 at Onawa by Christian K. Nelson, was the world's first chocolate-covered ice cream bar. It is still available in stores today.

Ff

is for
Fenelon Place
Elevator

Sometimes called the Fourth Street Elevator, it is one of the world's shortest and steepest inclined railways. Today you can still take rides on it. From the top of the bluffs, you can see a beautiful view of Dubuque and the Mississippi River.

Gg

is for
Grant Wood

Grant Wood was born near Anamosa and became one of America's famous artists. His painting "American Gothic" is recognized by many people as a masterpiece of art.

Hh

is for

Herbert Hoover

Herbert Hoover was born in West Branch and served as the thirty-first president of the United States.

He was the first president born west of the Mississippi River. There is a presidential library at the site of his birth.

Ii

is for
Indian
mounds

Early Indian settlers in Iowa built burial mounds to house their dead. These hills of earth were built in the shapes of animals and birds. The largest group of hills is known as Effigy Mounds and can still be seen near Marquette.

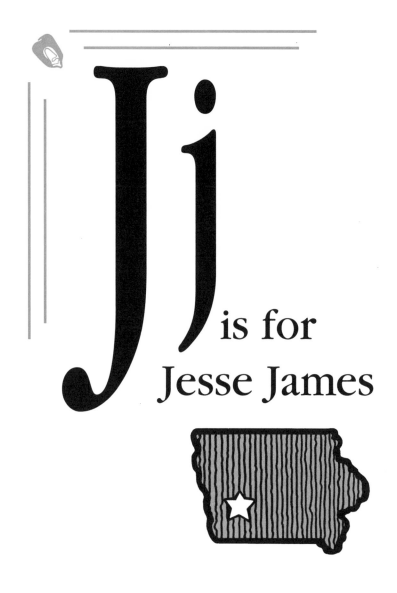

Jj

is for
Jesse James

Jesse James was one of America's most-famous outlaws. Together with his brother Frank, they led a gang of men who carried out the first train robbery in Adair, over 100 years ago.

Kk is for klokkenspel

Located at Franklin Place in Pella, this Dutch-styled musical clock has eight figures that represent the town's history. The klokkenspel is set for the figures to perform at certain hours.

This clock is one of only three such animated musical town clocks in the United States.

L1 is for Living History Farms

These working farms, located near Des Moines, show visitors about farm life in Iowa in the 1800s, the 1900s, and into the future.

Mm

is for

Maytag

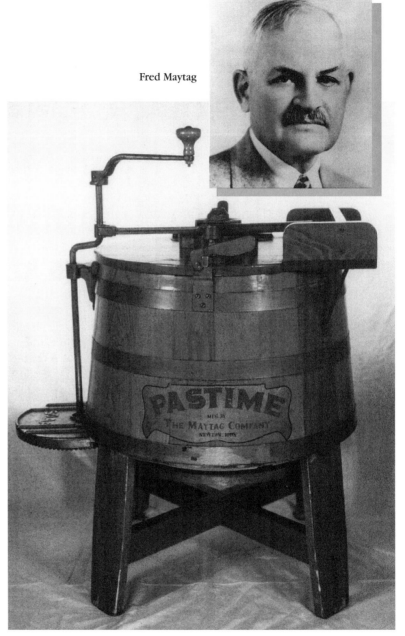

Fred Maytag

Fred Maytag introduced his first clothes washer in Newton in 1907. Newton has become the washing machine capital of the world. Maytag washers and dryers are still manufactured and sold today.

Nn
is for
nickname

One of Iowa's nicknames is "The Land Where the Tall Corn Grows." Iowa is the number-one producer of corn in the nation. Today there are hundreds of uses for corn or corn products—from food for people and animals, to crayons, to shoe polish, to ethanol for cleaner gasoline.

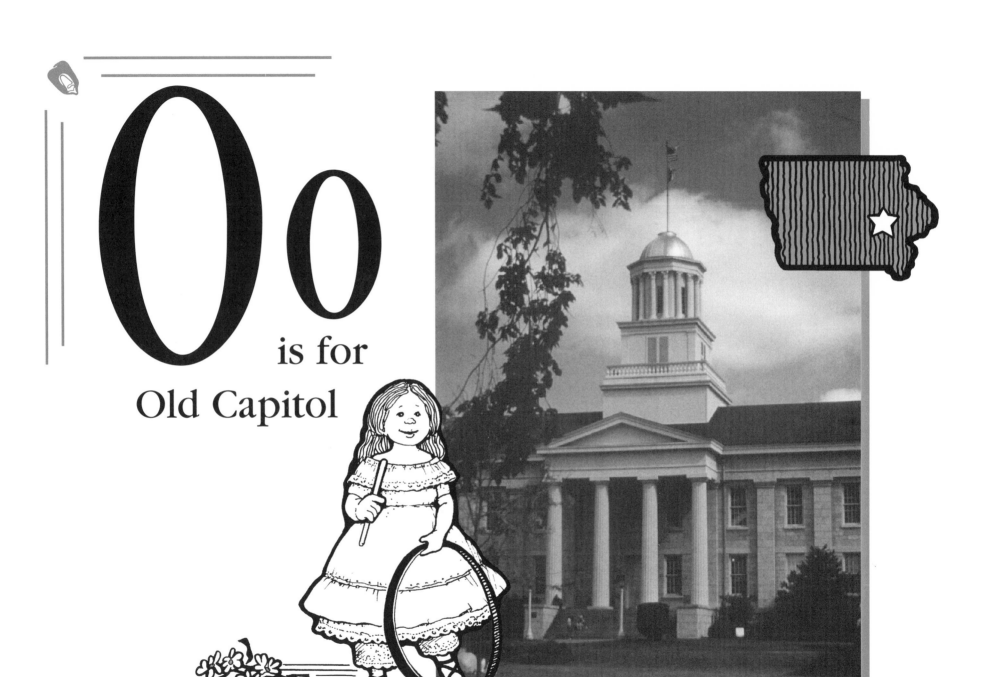

O o

is for

Old Capitol

Built in 1842, this building was the statehouse for the young state government until 1857. It has a golden dome and a beautiful winding staircase. The Old Capitol is a national historic landmark in Iowa City. Today the

statehouse is located in Des Moines.

Pp

is for

palaces

Bluegrass Palace
Creston, Iowa

Coal Palace
Ottumwa, Iowa

Corn Palace
Sioux City, Iowa

32

In the 1800s, the people of Iowa built grand palaces out of coal, bluegrass, corn, and other products as memorials to the crops they raised. These buildings represented a measure of the farmers' successes. The fertile land of Iowa produced bountiful harvests.

Qq is for
Quaker Oats

QUAKER

In the late 1800s, this company started in Cedar Rapids as one small factory. It has grown to be the largest cereal-producing factory in the world. The trademark, the Quaker man, stands for quality, purity, and honesty, the values of the company.

Rr

is for

Ringling

brothers

The Ringling brothers, three of whom were born in McGregor, formed the Ringling Brothers Circus. It later combined with the Barnum and Bailey Circus and was billed as "The Greatest Show on Earth." This circus still performs across America.

Ss is for
Snake Alley

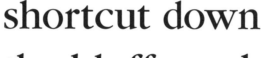

Located in Burlington, this street is called the "crookedest street in the world." It winds back and forth seven times in 275 feet. It was built as a shortcut down the bluffs to the  business district along the Mississippi River.

Tt

is for

Terrace Hill

This well-preserved Victorian mansion in Des Moines has been the home of Iowa governors since 1971.

The state flag flies beneath the American flag from the tower. Terrace Hill is open to the public for tours.

Uu

is for

underground

railway

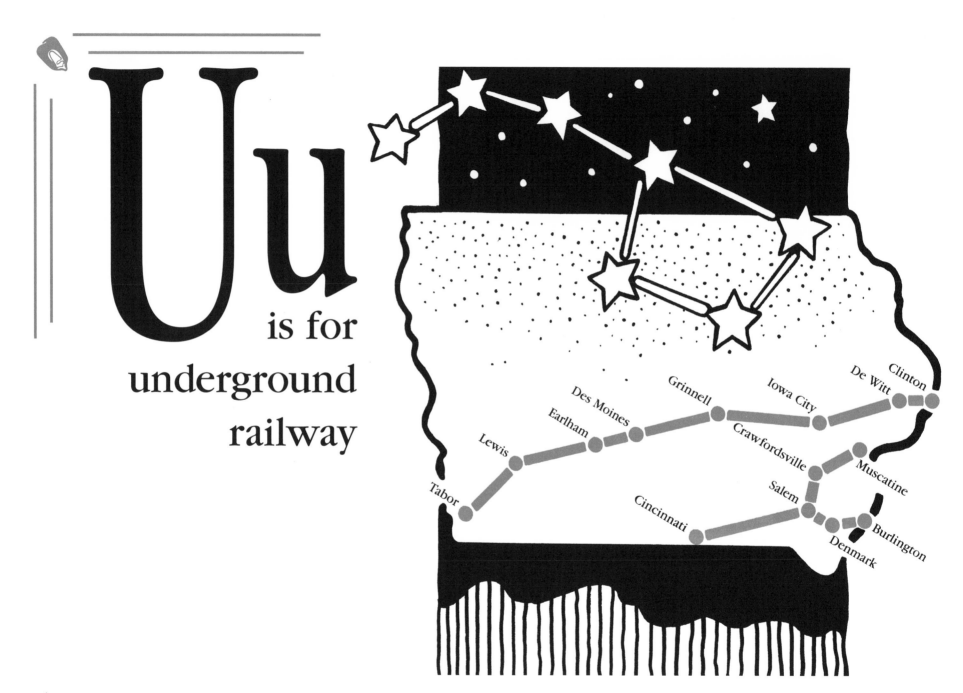

This term does not refer to a real railroad but rather to a system that was used to help escaped slaves reach a safe place.  The slaves traveled at night guided by the stars. They hid during the day, sometimes in secret places in people's homes.

Vv

is for vale

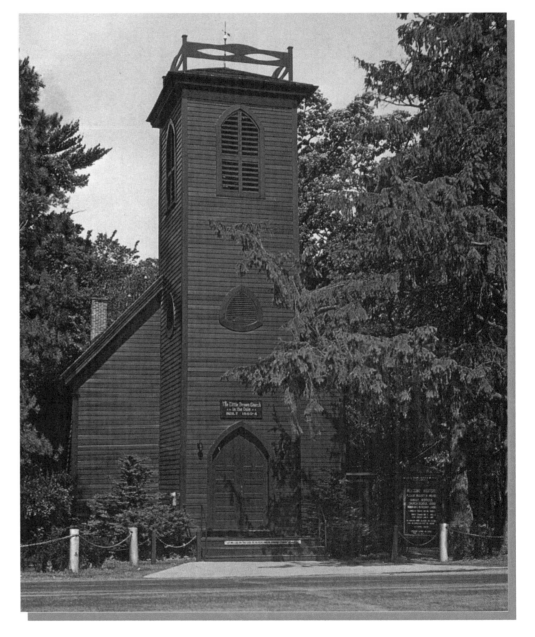

A vale is a small valley. In 1864, a small brown church was built in Nashua on the spot that inspired the hymn "The Church in the Wildwood." In the song, the church is called "the little brown church in the vale."

Ww

is for

Wallace

Henry A. Wallace, born in Adair County, was secretary of agriculture and then became Iowa's only vice president of the United States. He served under President Franklin D. Roosevelt.

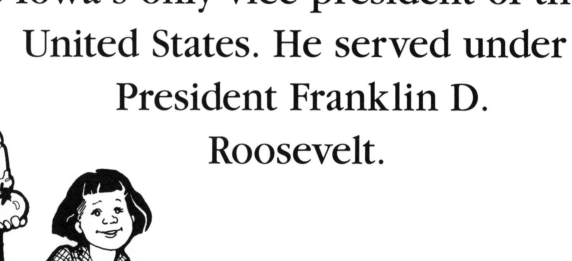

X x is for
X-ray
treatment

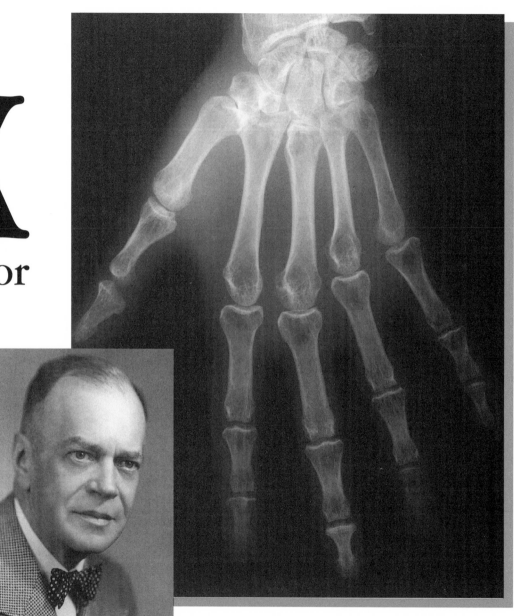

Arthur Erskine

48

X-ray treatment for cancer was first developed by Arthur Erskine. He was known worldwide as a respected doctor and researcher, who practiced medicine in Cedar Rapids between 1912 and 1954.

Yy is for
Yellow River
State Forest

Located in Allamakee County, this forest is popular for year-round recreation. Within the forest there are trout streams, wildlife, a state-owned sawmill, pioneer farm buildings, and hiking and snowmobile trails.

Zz
is for

Zebulon Pike

While exploring the Mississippi, Zebulon Pike recommended the hill known today as Pike's Peak as a site for an American fort. Iowa claims the *original* Pike's Peak, since this one had been named before the famous mountain in Colorado was discovered.

Behold the Work of the Old ...

Let your Heritage not be lost.

But bequeath it as a Memory,

Treasure and Blessing ...

Gather the lost and hidden

And preserve it for thy Children.

Christian Metz, 1846

Iowa history in an alphabet format—what better way to reach the minds of young children than through the letters with which they are familiar? Targeted at an audience of six- to ten-year-old children, this alphabet book provides a source of information about the state—geographical locations, industries, significant historical events, and extraordinary personalities. It helps any child who reads it or hears it, or looks at its pictures, to understand that Iowa's past was different from today, yet people still had hopes and dreams, fears and problems. It also implies that important decisions were made in the past that affect our lives now. The words and pictures work together to highlight historical facts that are representative of the state's diversity and heritage.

It is my belief that many historical concepts are already familiar to young children, and they have the capability of learning new facts that are presented in a meaningful way. *I is for Iowa* places primary focus on introducing historical concepts. It is historically accurate as well as currently relevant to all who live in or pass through Iowa.

The book is designed to stimulate language development and to help young children become interested in reading and in learning more about the state of Iowa. As a source of information for the teacher who tackles the challenge of striving to help children understand the connection between the present and the past, *I is for Iowa* is also an important tool to assist educators in developing their Iowa history units to meet the needs and interests of children. For young children, there is a definite shortage of books in print that pertain to the history of Iowa. This alphabet book fills an obvious gap in state historical literature. Hopefully it will set its readers, regardless of age, on a path of exploration to learn more about the history of the state we call Iowa.

The selection of a single concept for each letter was a challenge. There are simply too many facts, places, and personalities in Iowa's history to choose one concept and a picture to adorn each letter in the alphabet. What I have included will provide a unique look at Iowa's history. An attempt was made to exclude the more-common topics that could be fairly easily found in reference books. Criteria for inclusion was importance to the past and/or relevancy to the present. The featured industries continue to help shape the economy of the state. The geographic locations are places currently open to the public for visitation. I feel certain that the selected concepts and photos make a book that many children and adults will learn from and enjoy.

The idea for this book came about as a result of teaching early childhood classes and never being able to find a book to share with my students about the state of Iowa that was appropriate for their age and grade level. I needed a book that would introduce my students to the rich history of Iowa and encourage further investigation of topics related to those in the book. I hope the readers will discover something of interest that will lead to further exploration about past and present Iowa. *I is for Iowa* is a resource for teachers, librarians, parents, grandparents, and young readers alike. Between its covers each person will discover fascinating facts about Iowa's history!

Many people deserve to be thanked for their part in the creation of this book. First, I am grateful to my parents for teaching me to value education. The next acknowledgment goes to my husband Steve, who supported my decision to attend graduate school. This permitted me the opportunity to write *I is for Iowa* as a research project. He provided the encouragement and computer assistance needed to bring this book into being.

My daughter Anne and my son Christopher both took an active part in searching for, screening, and helping select intriguing and relevant topics to represent the state. A big thank-you goes to them for the enthusiasm they have shared with me about the book.

A most sincere thank-you goes to my professors in graduate school at the University of Northern Iowa, Dr. Leah Hiland and Dr. Barbara Safford, for the wisdom they shared with me and for their encouragement.

I am grateful to numerous professional people throughout the state for helping me locate photographic images that were essential to this book. I also give thanks to others who discussed various aspects of Iowa history with me and made certain that the text of the book was historically accurate.

Finally, I would like to thank the staff at Iowa State University Press for seeing the vision I had for this book and for understanding my desire to teach children about the state of Iowa. Through their willingness to publish this book, my vision has become real.

Photograph Acknowledgments

Grateful acknowledgment is expressed to the following for permission to reprint their photographs:

Aa: Amana Heritage Society
Bb: State Historical Society of Iowa, Iowa City
Cc: Iowa State University/University Archives
Dd: State Historical Society of Iowa, Iowa City
Ee: Eskimo Pie Corporation
Ff: James L. Shaffer
Gg: The Art Institute of Chicago; Malcolm D. McMichael
Hh: Herbert Hoover Presidential Library
Ii: U.S. Department of Interior, National Park Service
Jj: Missouri Historical Society
Kk: Pella Chamber of Commerce
Ll: Greater Des Moines Convention and Visitors Bureau
Mm: Maytag Corporation
Nn: Iowa Department of Economic Development
Oo: Iowa Department of Economic Development
Pp: State Historical Society of Iowa, Iowa City
Qq: The Quaker Oats Company
Rr: Courtesy of Circus World Museum, Baraboo, Wisconsin; reproduced by permission of Ringling Bros.–Barnum & Bailey Combined Shows, Inc.
Ss: Iowa Department of Economic Development
Tt: Greater Des Moines Convention and Visitors Bureau
Uu: Author, Mary Ann Gensicke
Vv: The Little Brown Church in the Vale
Ww: Iowa State University Press
Xx: Arthur Erskine, Bernice Prunskunas; X ray, St. Luke's Hospital, Cedar Rapids, Iowa
Yy: Bob Honeywell
Zz: Colorado Historical Society